PETE & MOE™

Visit

PROFESSOR SWIZZLE'S

ROBOTS

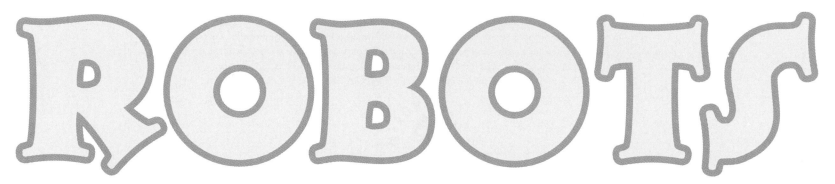

BY VINCENT GIARRANO

Published by Dark Horse Comics, Inc., 10956 Southeast Main Street, Milwaukie, Oregon 97222.

ISBN: 1-56971-007-4
First edition: November 1993
Printed in Canada

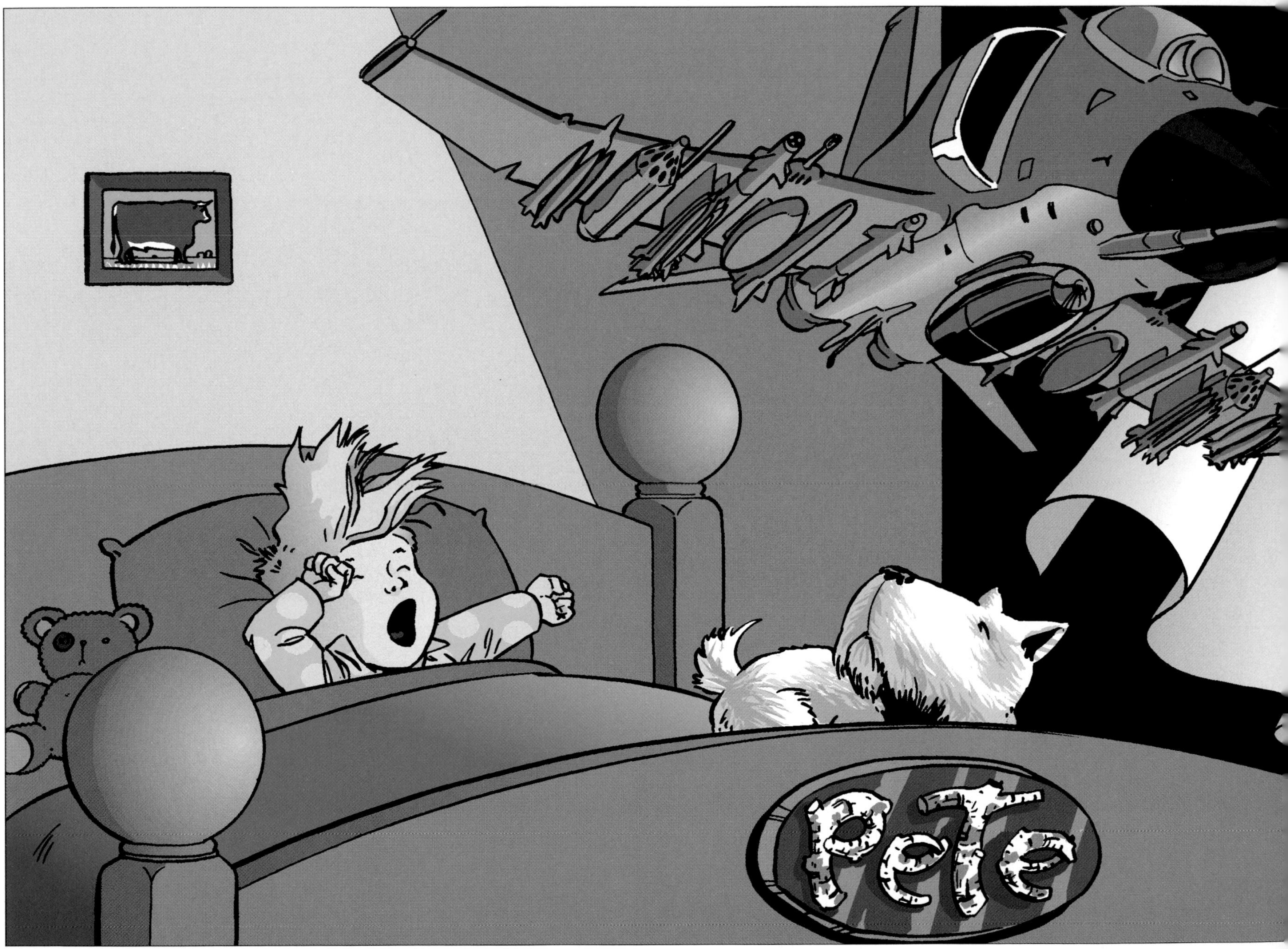
PeTe

My dog Moe and I got up very early today because we are going to visit our good friend Professor Swizzle. He's been working on something special to be in today's big parade and has invited us to his laboratory to see it.

After breakfast we started off.
It looked like a perfect day for the
parade: no rain clouds, just the big
fluffy kind. Moe doesn't care much for
clouds, but I like to see how many
shapes I can find in them.

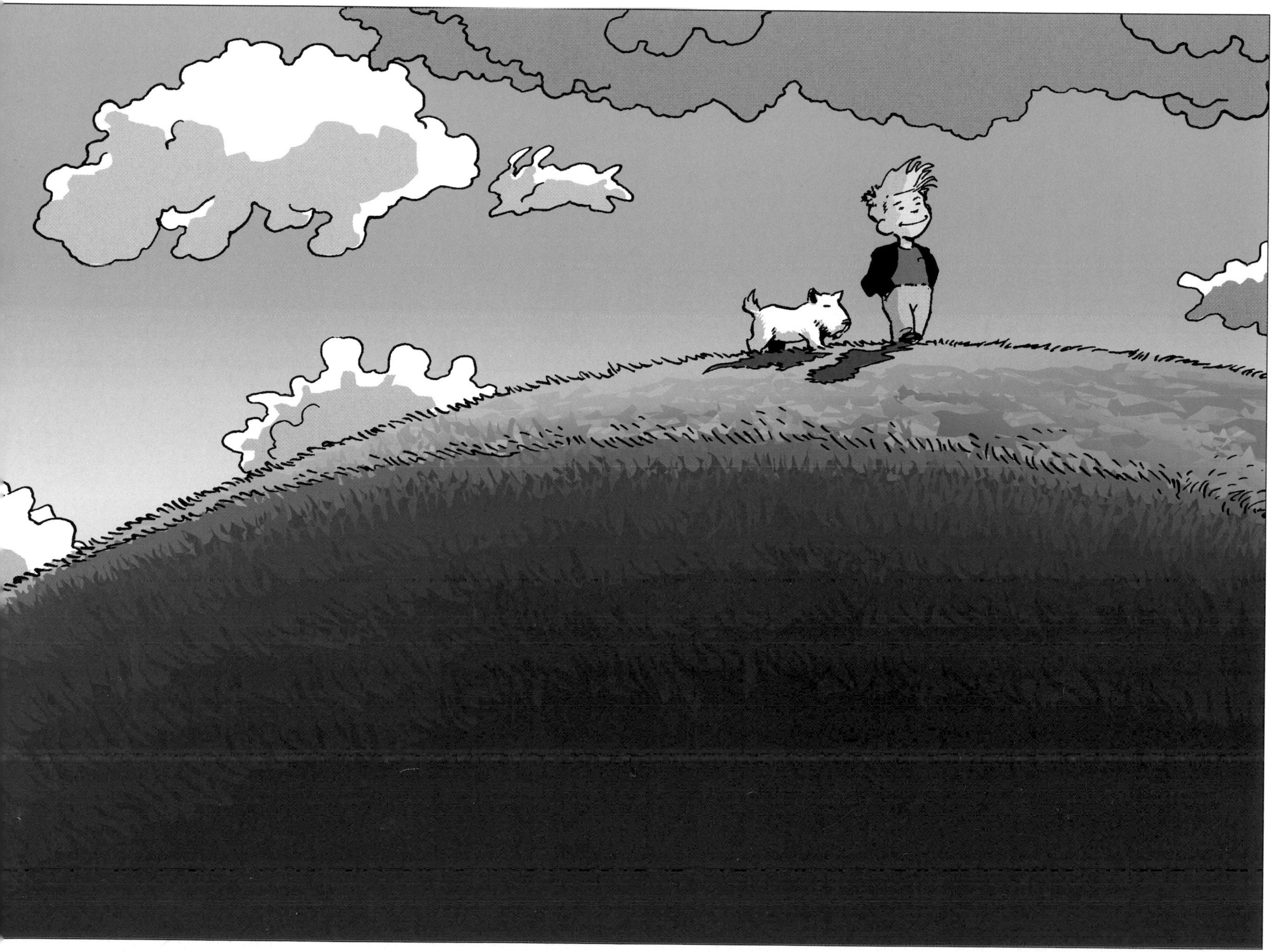

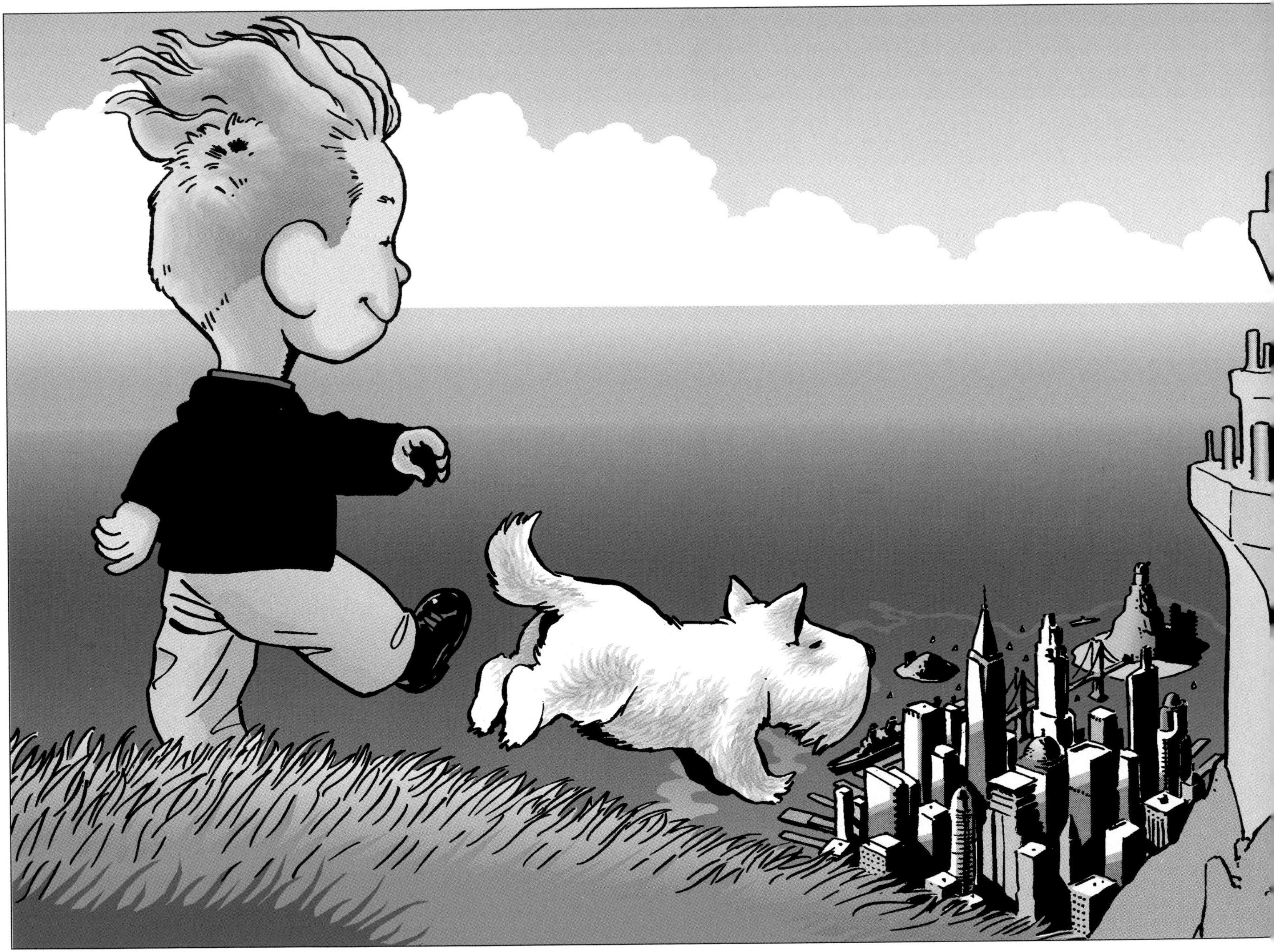

From the top of the hill
we could finally see Professor
Swizzle's laboratory. No one's
quite sure how it was built —
it just seemed to be there
one day.

When we reached the giant doorway I knocked as hard as I could — Boom! Boom! Boom! — and Moe barked a couple of times for good measure. After a few minutes, the professor's doorman, Rusty, greeted us.

I said, "Hello, Rusty, is the professor in?" As usual he said nothing and led us in.

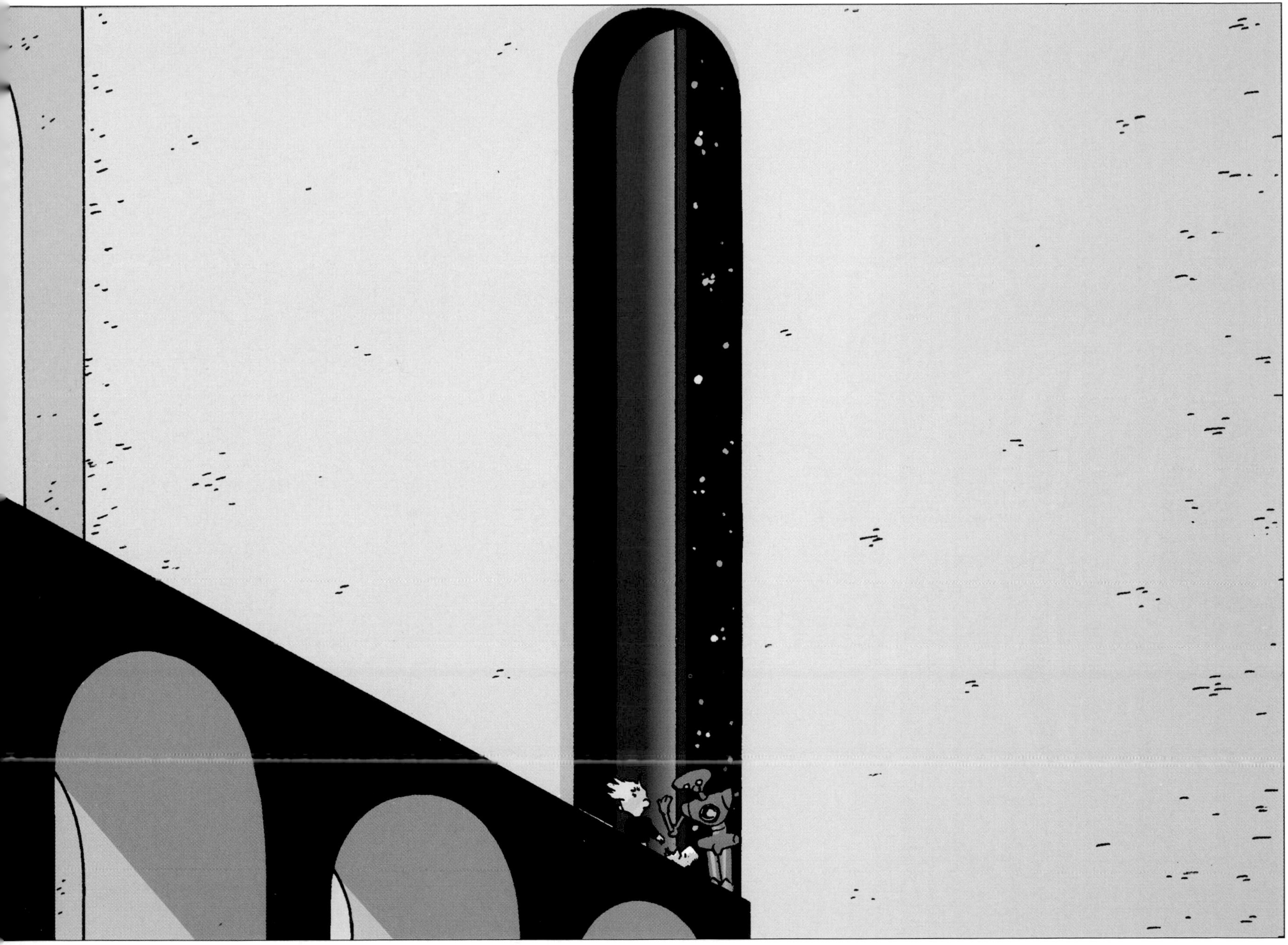

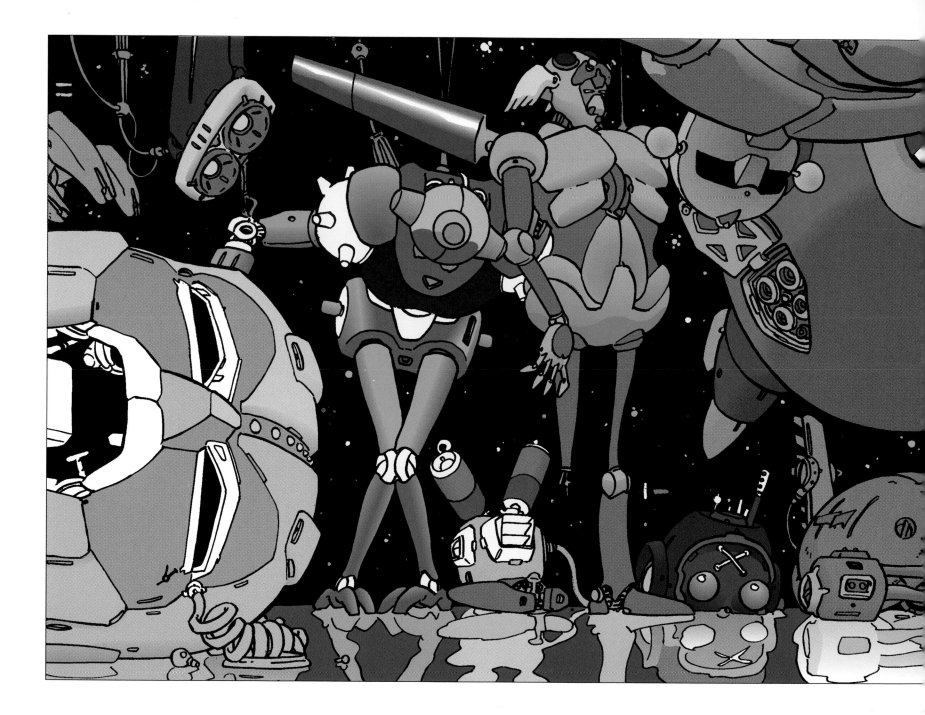

I think Professor Swizzle has about as many different robots as you could imagine. There are all sorts of shapes, sizes, and colors. I don't think I've seen them all, because there are just too many to count, but the professor keeps making more.

"How are you doing today, Professor?" I said as we approached.

"Well, hello, Pete! And hello, Moe!" he said. "I'm doing just fine but I need my hammer and I left it over there."

"Don't worry — I'll get it," I said.

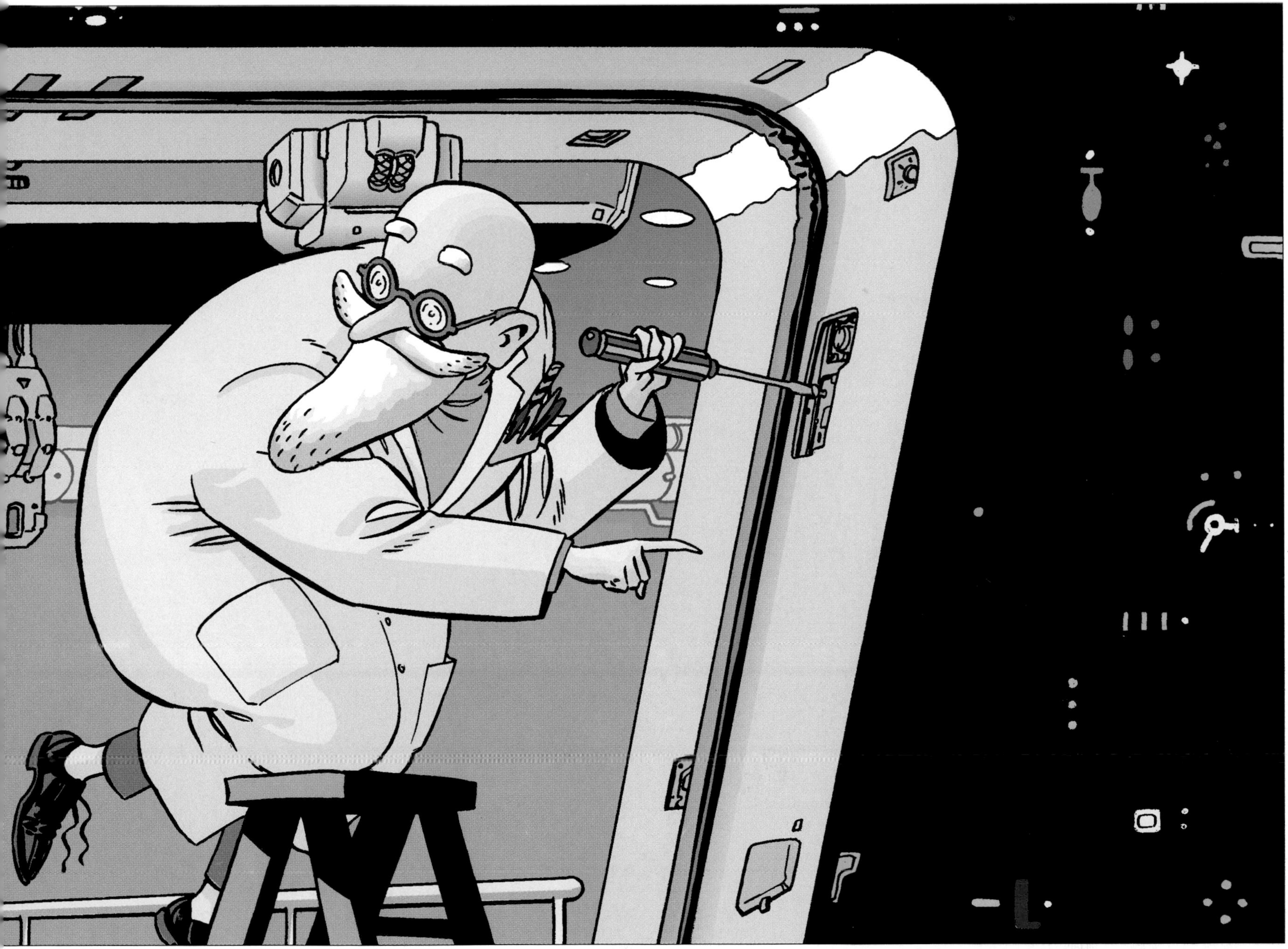

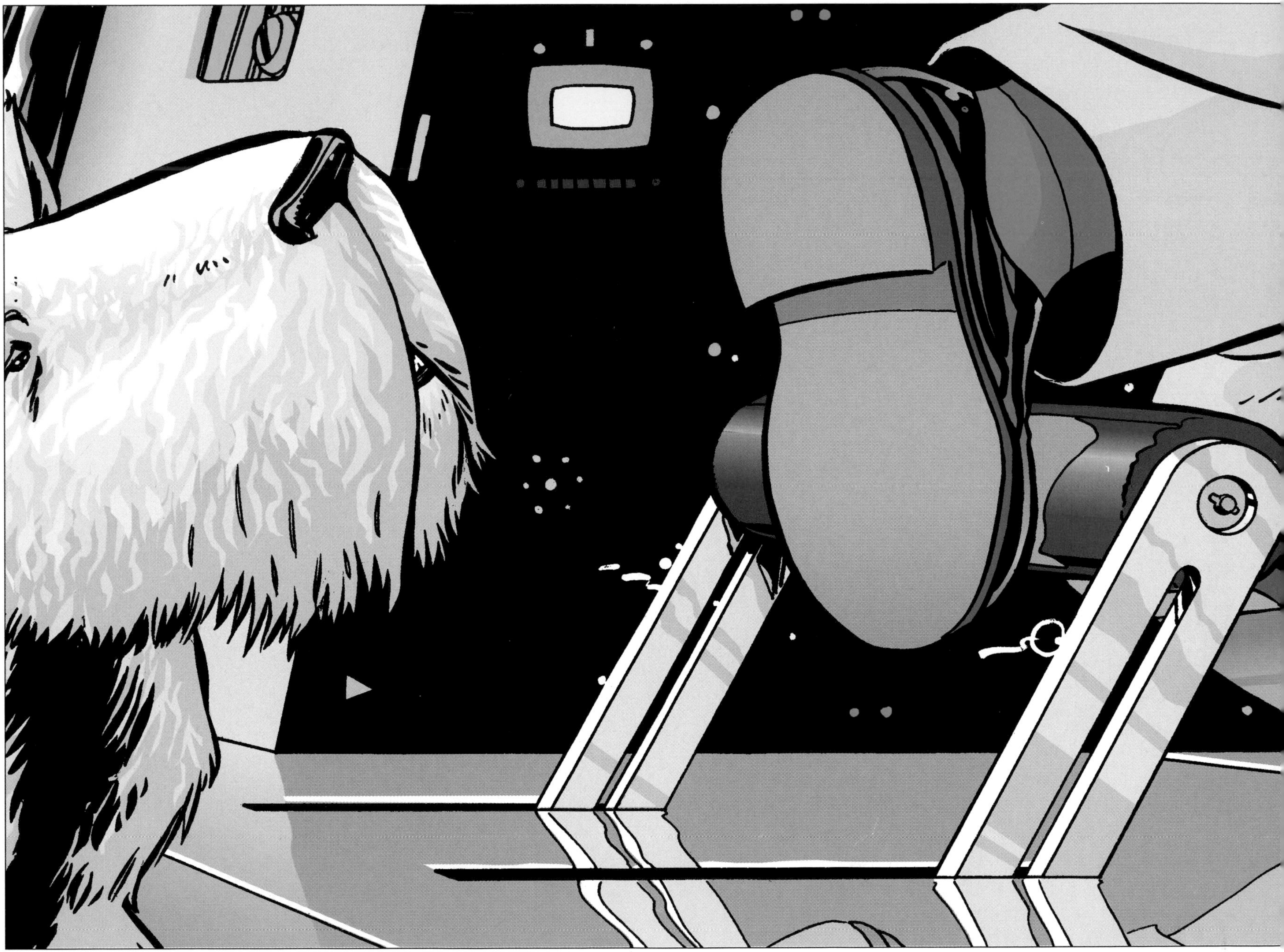

"Be careful not to trip on that switch," the professor warned, but it was too late. A deep humming noise seemed to come from all around, and the once dark room became filled with many tiny lights.

"Yeow! Come back!" the professor exclaimed, as Moe and I were carried off in a huge robot. With a loud crash the robot broke through the laboratory wall.

"Help, Professor!" I yelled.

"Bark! Bark!" cried Moe, but we kept moving farther and farther away.

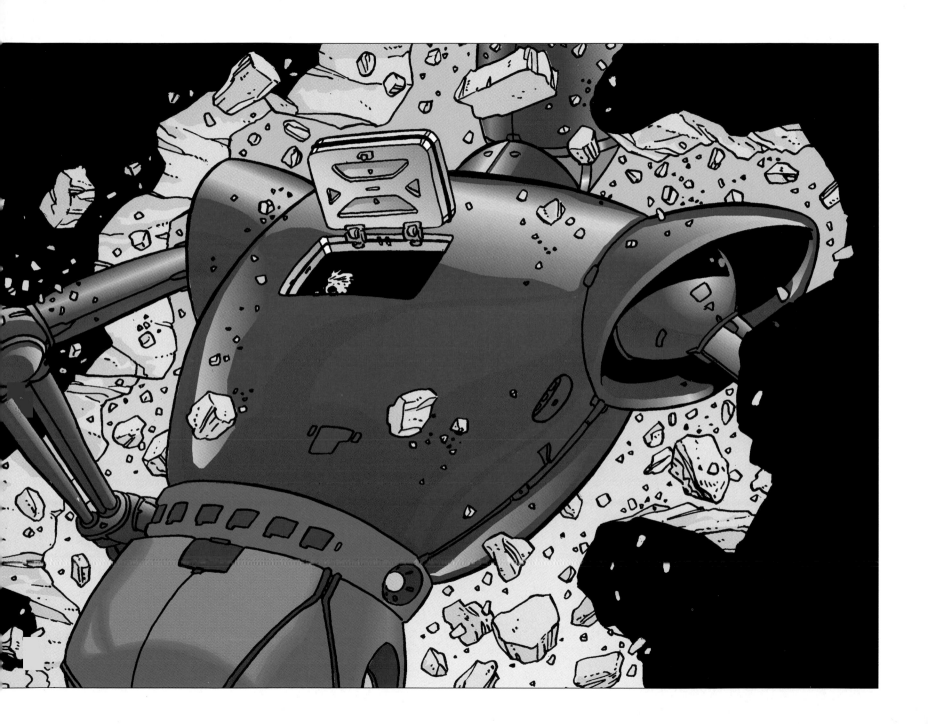

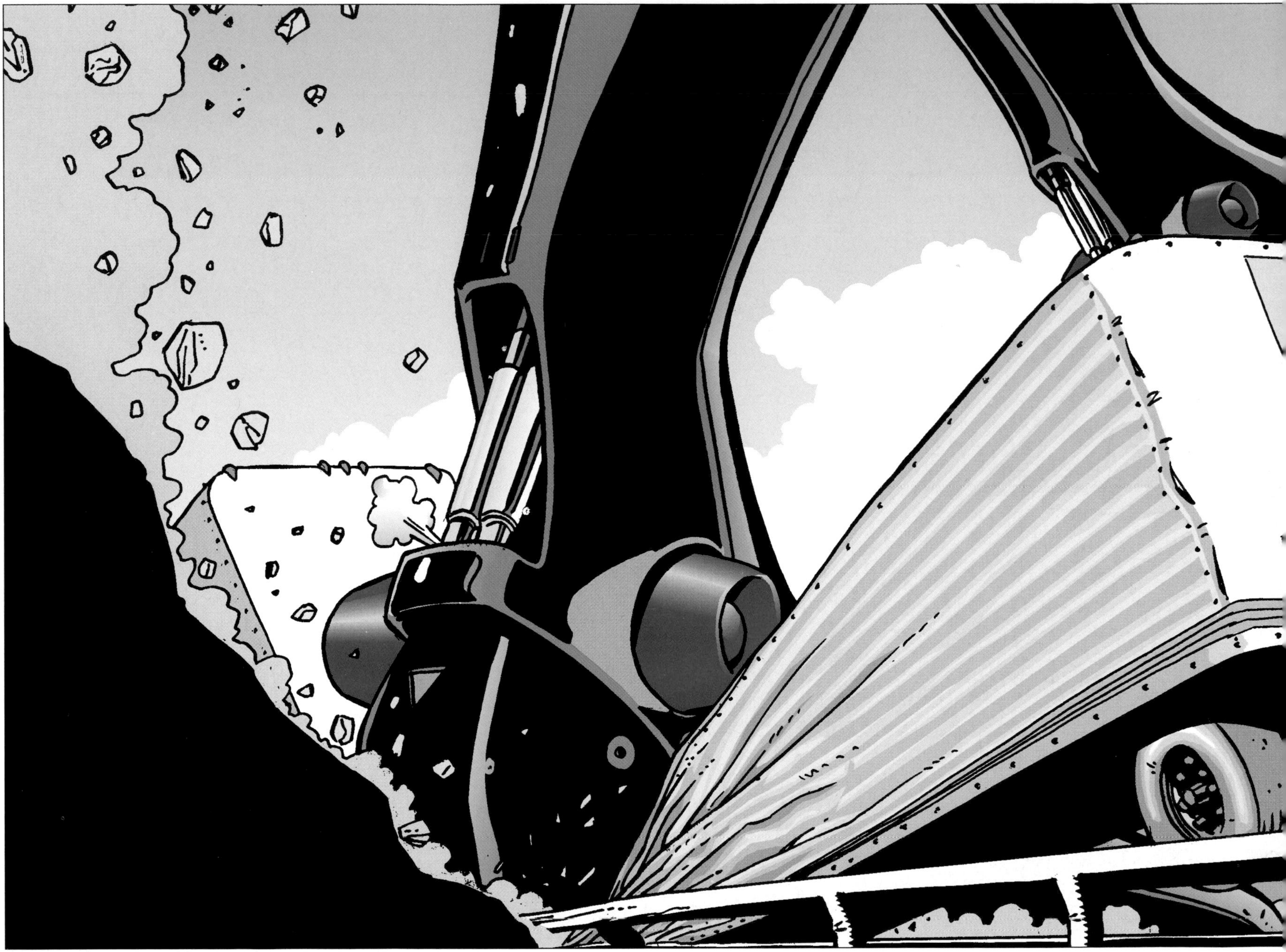

Down the hill and over the highway we went, crushing everything that stood in our way. Moe and I were helpless inside the giant mechanical monster. I knew that somehow we must try and stop it before it reached the defenseless city.

Moe barked at me to push the levers, but they were too big for me to move. Moe would have really been upset if he could have seen the buildings getting closer and closer.

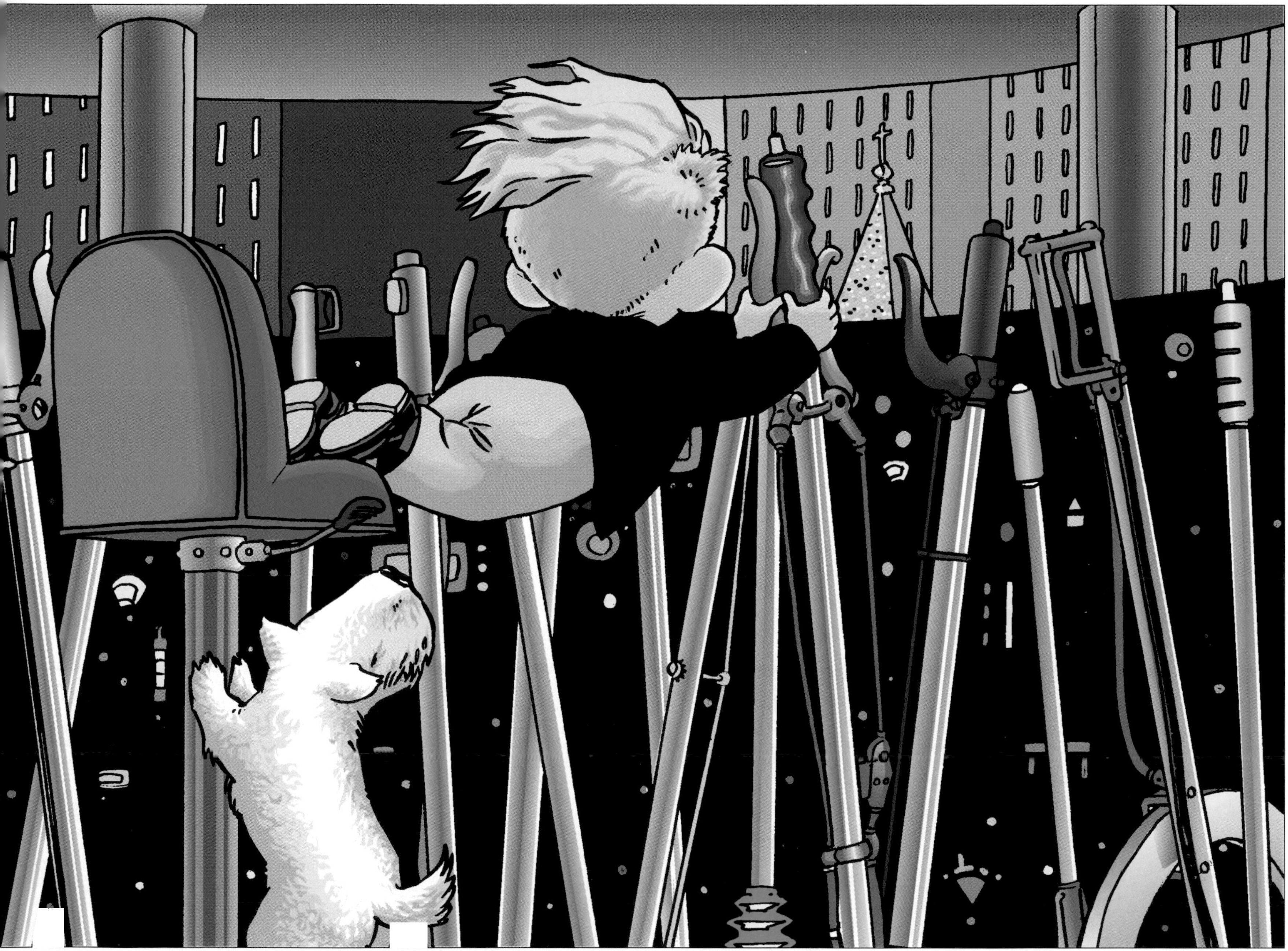

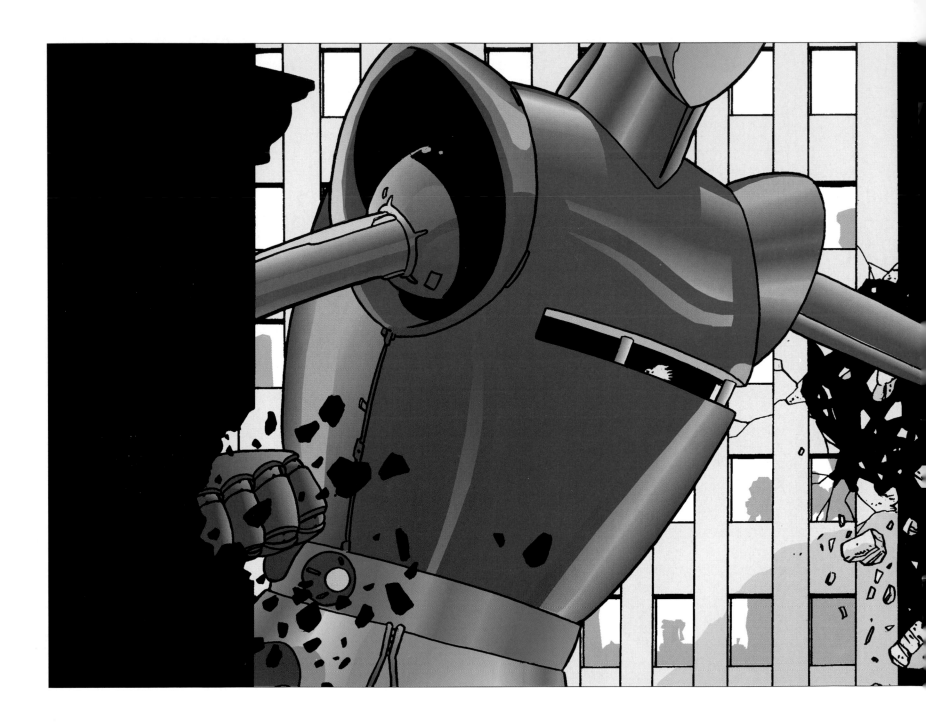

The robot plunged into the city with its great metal arms swinging. It smashed and crumbled building after building as it strode down Main Street.

Suddenly, the great robot stopped. When Moe and I climbed out, there we saw Professor Swizzle. He had deactivated the robot and saved the city.

"My, what a mess," he said. "We must fix all this in time for the parade." With that he pressed a small button on his belt and said, "My worker robots should do nicely, I think."

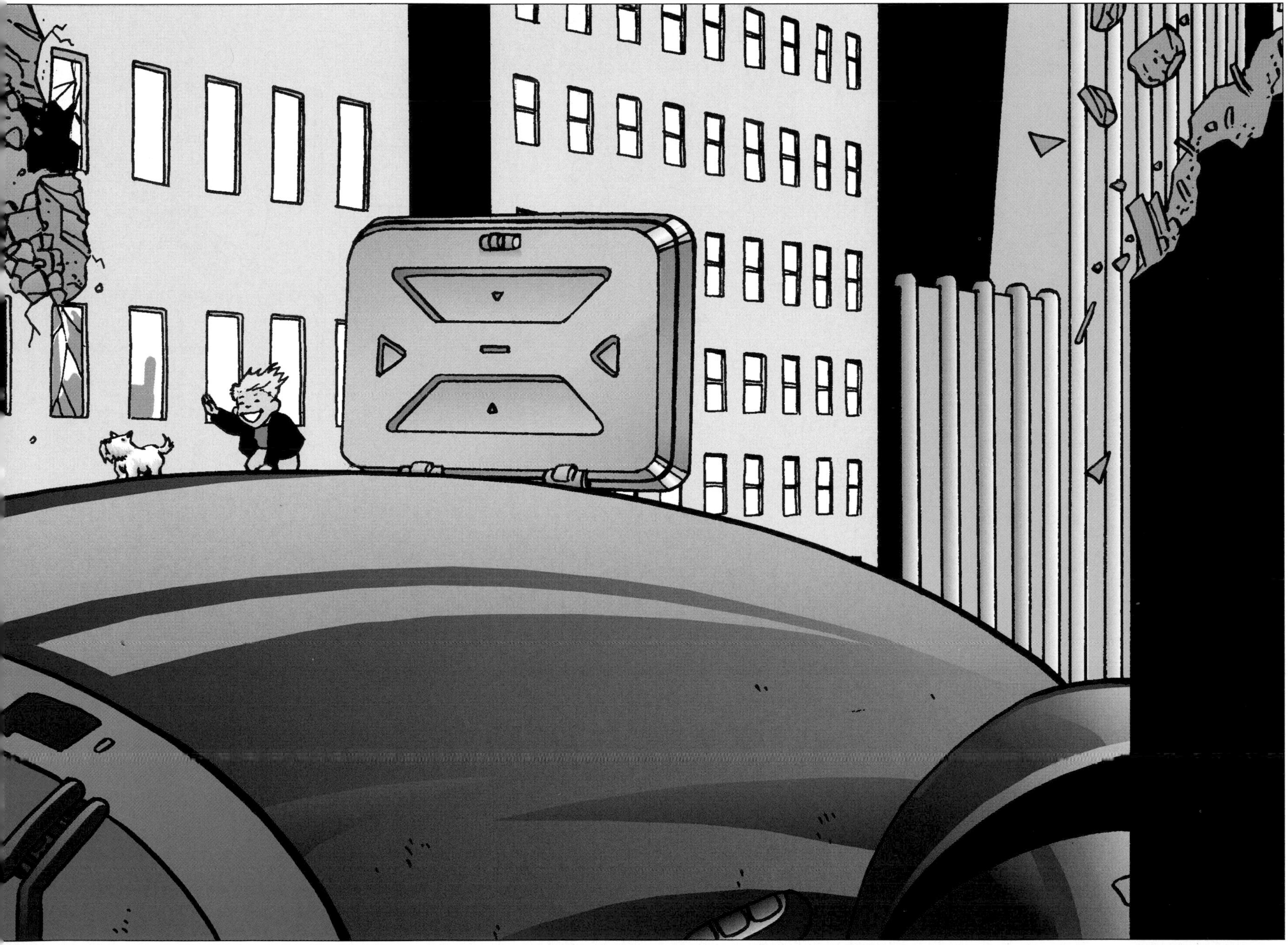

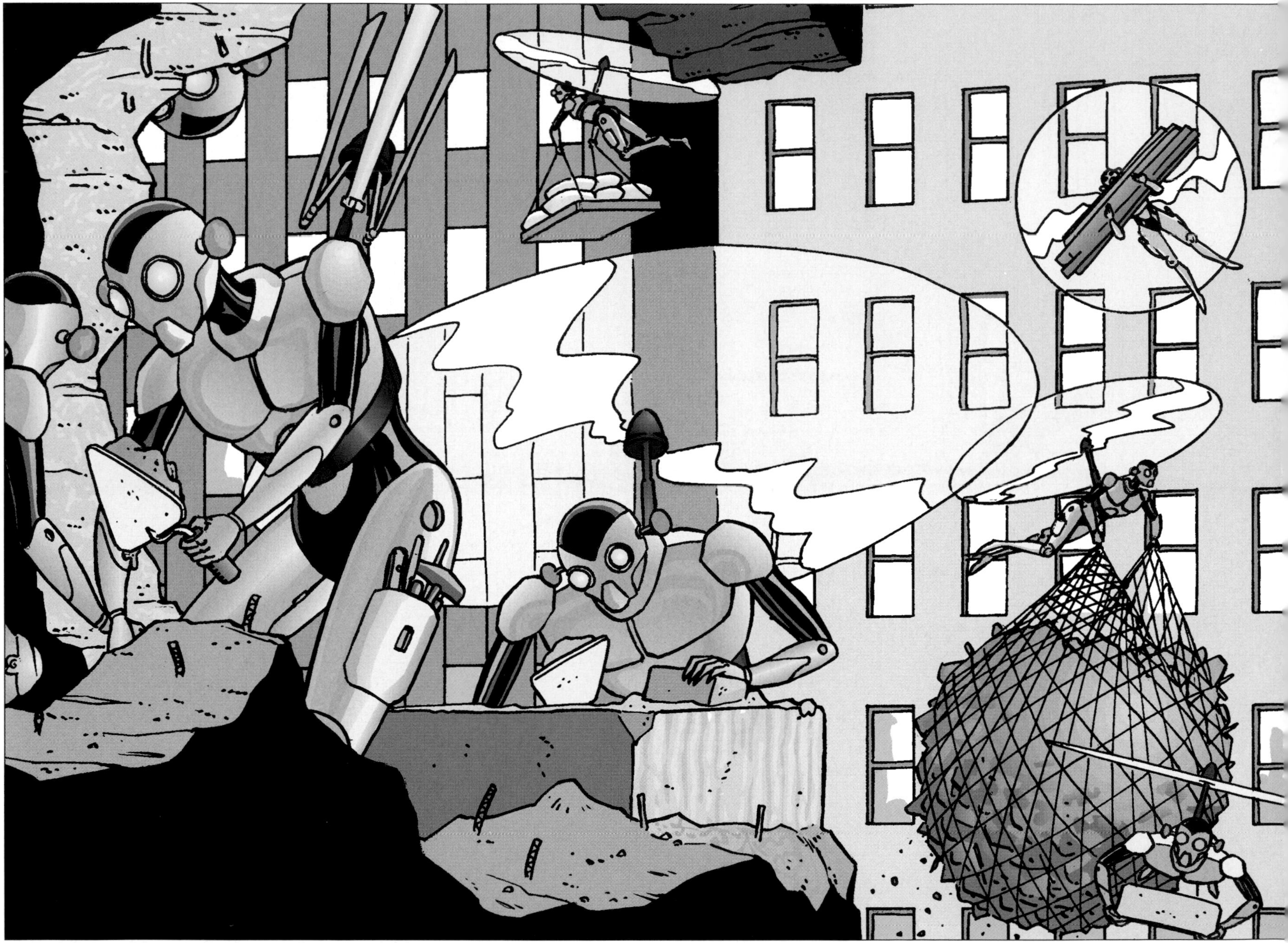

Soon the sky was filled with many small robots who immediately began to work on repairing the city. While Moe and I stayed to watch them, the professor took the giant robot back to his laboratory.

With amazing speed the worker robots completed their task in time for the big parade. Crowds of people lined the street and cheered as we passed. Professor Swizzle's giant robot was a success after all.

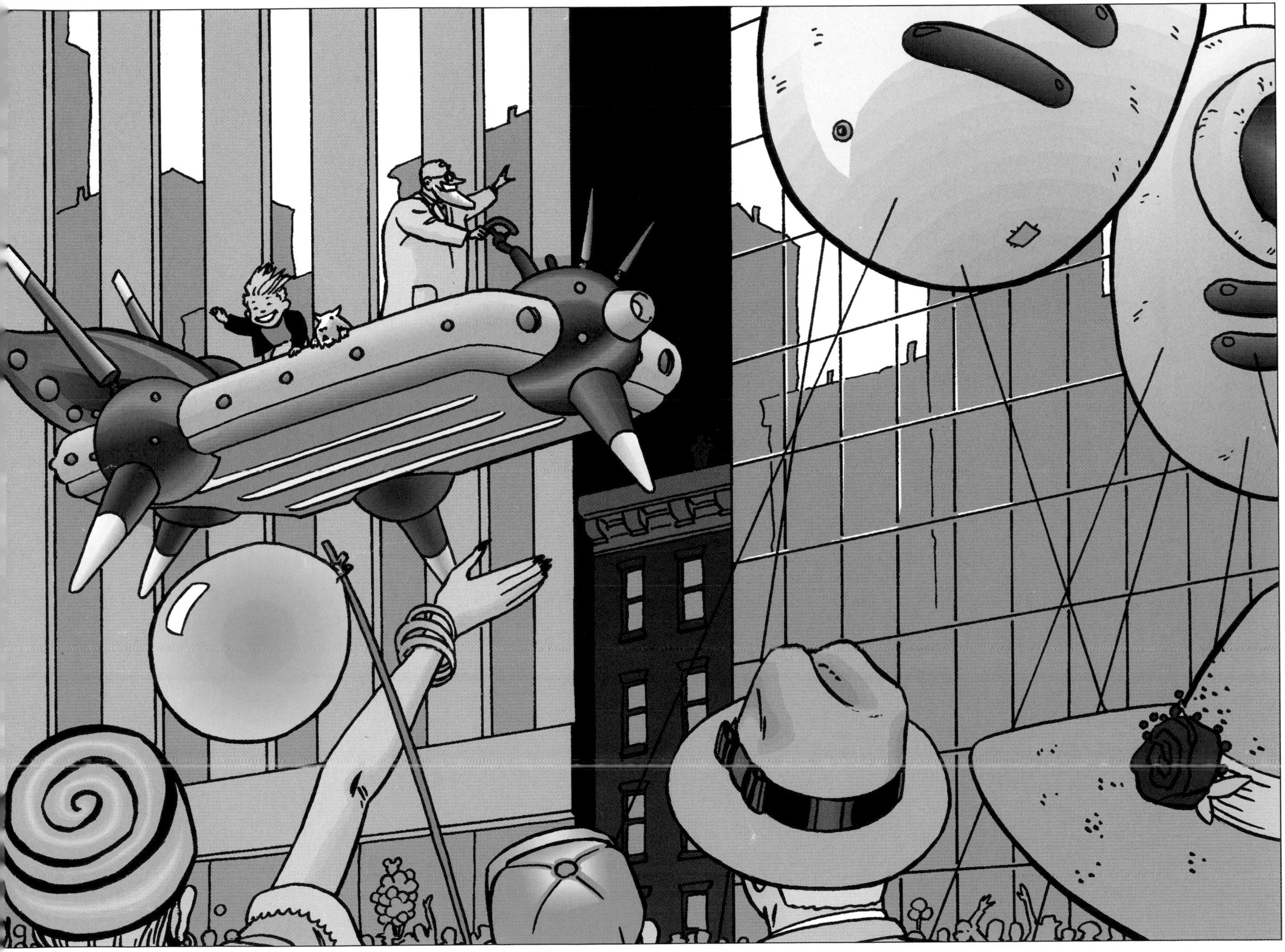

THE END